BIG CATS

AN IMAGINATION
LIBRARY SERIES

COUGARS

by Victor Gentle and Janet Perry

Gareth Stevens Publishing
A WORLD ALMANAC EDUCATION GROUP COMPANY

Please visit our web site at: www.garethstevens.com
For a free color catalog describing Gareth Stevens Publishing's
list of high-quality books and multimedia programs,
call 1-800-542-2595 or fax your request to (414) 332-3567.

Library of Congress Cataloging-in-Publication Data

Gentle, Victor.
    Cougars / by Victor Gentle and Janet Perry.
       p. cm. — (Big cats: an imagination library series)
    Includes bibliographical references and index.
    Summary: An introduction to the physical characteristics, behavior, and natural environment
of the cougar or puma, a wild cat of the Americas that continues to decline in number.
    ISBN 0-8368-3025-3 (lib. bdg.)
    1. Puma—Juvenile literature. [1. Puma.] I. Perry, Janet, 1960- II. Title.
QL737.C23G47   2002
599.75'24—dc21   2001049693

First published in 2002 by
Gareth Stevens Publishing
A World Almanac Education Group Company
330 West Olive Street, Suite 100
Milwaukee, WI 53212 USA

Text: Victor Gentle and Janet Perry
Page layout: Victor Gentle, Janet Perry, and Tammy Gruenewald
Cover design: Tammy Gruenewald
Series editor: Catherine Gardner
Picture Researcher: Diane Laska-Swanke

Photo credits: Cover, pp. 5, 7 (inset), 9, 13 © Tom & Pat Leeson; pp. 7 (main), 11, 15, 17, 21
© Alan & Sandy Carey; p. 19 © David Welling/BBC Natural History Unit

Printed in the United States of America

1 2 3 4 5 6 7 8 9 06 05 04 03 02

Front cover: A mother and her two cubs.
The cubs are growing fast. It won't be long
before they leave her to hunt on their own.

TABLE OF CONTENTS

Words that appear in the glossary are printed in **boldface** type the first time they occur in the text.

BEETLEJUICE TO MOOSE MEAT

What animal eats mice, porcupines, deer, and moose? What leaps to tree branches as high as the tallest truck? What lives in dry deserts, snowy mountains, and tropical rain forests? What screams but cannot roar? What has spots as a baby but none as an adult?

"A mountain lion," you say. Right! "A puma." Right! "A panther." Right again! This large wild cat has many names. In this book, we call this animal a "cougar."

This cougar in the western United States has caught a porcupine. Very, very carefully, the cougar pulls out the sharp quills before it eats its tricky treat.

ONE BIG KITTY

Cougars are some of the biggest wild cats living in North and South America. Only one kind of American wild cat — the **jaguar** — is bigger than a cougar.

Male cougars are bigger than females. Two males weigh as much as three females. Males can grow to more than 175 pounds (80 kilograms) and 7.2 feet (2.2 meters), head to tail. That is about the size of a professional basketball player!

In warm places, like Central America or Brazil, cougars are smaller than cougars that live in cooler places like Canada.

Cougars are any color from brownish red to silvery gray. Inset: Jaguars, the other big cats of the Americas, have spots.

HERE, THERE, EVERYWHERE

Cougars live all the way from Canada to the tip of South America. They survive in many kinds of **habitats**. Cougars like the cover of trees and shrubs, but they can live in open deserts and grasslands.

Most cougars live far from towns and cities. Most cougars prefer to stay away from people — and even from other cougars. Some, however, live near people's homes. This makes some people very nervous.

This cougar lives in the woodlands of Canada and the northern United States.

HOME ALONE

Adult cougars live alone for much of their lives. They hunt alone, they eat alone, and they sleep alone. A male and a female get together for only a few days to **mate**.

When a mother cougar has **cubs**, she looks after them for up to two years. She feeds them, protects them, and teaches them to hunt. She raises the cubs alone, without help from the father or other females. When the young cougars can take care of themselves, they leave their family and live alone.

For safety, a mother cougar moves her cubs often. This careful mom quickly carries a cub to a safer place.

HIDING SPOTS

A mother cougar has one to six cubs at one time. She keeps her cubs in a **den**. The den may be in a thick clump of bushes, in a jumble of rocks, or under an uprooted tree. These are all good hiding places.

The cubs have spotted fur, which helps them hide. The spots make it hard for **predators** to see the cubs. Cougar cubs have many enemies. Even their father might kill them, if he found them!

For six weeks, cubs feed on their mother's milk. Then, she hunts for meat to bring home to them.

A cougar feeds milk to two cubs. The third cub uses its mother's shoulders as a safe look-out post.

LEARNING TO HUNT, SAFELY

When a mother cougar brings meat to her cubs for the first time, they do not always know what to do with it. They attack it, play with it, or even back away from it. Finally, they get the idea. They chew on it! Then, the mother licks the cubs clean.

Later, the cubs go hunting with their mother. She teaches them to kill far away from where they sleep. Predators like wolves, coyotes, or other cougars may find the dead **prey** — and any cubs sleeping nearby.

These cubs are about two months old. Their play is part of their education. They are learning to hunt.

IT'S WHAT'S FOR DINNER

Like all big cats, cougars are skilled hunters. They are strong enough to kill a moose and quick enough to catch a mouse. Cougars usually choose prey that is easy to find and catch. In North America, deer is the favorite meal. North American cougars eat larger and smaller prey, too. Cougars in Central and South America chase small prey, like hares and **rodents**.

Sometimes, cougars hunt animals that are very rare. In western Canada, a few cougars eat **caribou**. But caribou are **endangered**, too!

This cougar has spotted a smaller snack — a red fox. Hungry cougars also hunt ground squirrels, birds, and beetles.

HUMANS AGAINST COUGARS

Farmers and hunters have killed most of the cougars in eastern North America. In western North America, only 15,000 cougars may be left in the wild.

The number of humans is growing fast. People build more homes next to the wilderness, and they destroy the habitat for cougars and their prey. As people live, work, and play closer to wild areas, people and cougars meet more often.

A cougar roaring? No, cougars do not roar. Cougars **yowl**. Yowling may sound scary, but it is just a message to faraway cougars, "Hi! I'm here."

COUGARS: TO KILL OR CARE FOR?

Cougars sometimes attack farm animals. A few cougars have even killed people. So, some people think cougars are pests. They want to kill all the wild cougars.

Cougars are important to the **balance of nature**. For example, cougars help keep prey animals healthy and strong by catching and eating the weaker ones. So, many people think cougars are not pests. They want cougars protected.

Will cougars and people find a way to live together? The way people answer that question will decide the future for cougars. Since we cannot ask cougars what *they* think, what do *you* think?

What kind of future is this cub looking at? Will its children or grandchildren be the last wild cougars?

MORE TO READ AND VIEW

Books (Nonfiction)
Big Cats (series). Victor Gentle and Janet Perry (Gareth Stevens)
Cats. Animals Are Not Like Us (series). Graham Meadows
  (Gareth Stevens)
Cougars. Lynn M. Stone (Lerner)
The Florida Panther. Alvin and Virginia Silverstein (Millbrook Press)
Rocky Mountain Seasons: From Valley to Mountaintop. Diane L. Burns
  (Atheneum)

Books (Fiction)
Little Lions. Jim Arnosky (Putnam)
Realm of the Panther. Emily Costello (Soundprints)

Videos (Nonfiction)
Cougar: Elusive Predator. Wild Encounters (series). (Karvonen Films)
Cougar: Ghost of the Rockies. World of Discovery (series). (ABC Video)
Curious Cougar Kittens. (Discovery Communications)
North America. Wild About Animals (series). (Madacy Entertainment)
Panther and Cougar. Audubon's Animal Adventures (series). (HBO)
Puma: Lion of the Andes. (National Geographic)

PLACES TO VISIT, WRITE, OR CALL

Cougars live at the following zoos. Call or write to the zoos to find out about their cougars and their plans to preserve cougars in the wild. Better yet, go see the cougars, person to cat!

Black Pine Animal Park
349 W. Albion Road
Albion, IN 46701
(219) 636-7383

Northwest Trek Wildlife Park
11610 Trek Drive East
Eatonville, WA 98328
(360) 832-6117

Homosassa Springs Wildlife State Park
4150 S. Suncoast Blvd. (US Highway 19)
Homosassa, FL 34446
(352) 628-2311

The Zoo in Forest Park
P.O. Box 80295
Springfield, MA 01138-0295
(413) 733-2251

WEB SITES

Web sites change frequently, but we believe the following web sites are going to last. You also can use a good search engine, such as **Yahooligans!** [*www.yahooligans.com*] or **Google** [*www.google.com*], to find more information about cougars, other big cats around the world, and their homes. Some keywords that will help are: *cougars, jaguars, pumas, American wildlife, zoo animals,* and *endangered species.*

www.yahooligans.com
Yahooligans! is a great research tool. It has a lot of information and plenty to do. Under Science and Nature, click on Animals and then click on The Big Picture: Animals. From there, you can try Animal Videos, Endangered Animals, Animal Bytes, BBC Animals, or Natural History Notebooks and search for information on cougars, forests, mountains, and American wildlife.

www.leopardsetc.com/meet.html
Leopards, Etc. lets you hear big cats. Click on the speaker icon next to each cat's name. You can hear all kinds of big cats roaring, growling, rasping, barking, and purring.

www.nationalgeographic.com/features/97/cats/
National Geographic has a really cool game that lets you design the perfect predator.

www.nhm.org/cats/
The Natural History Museum of Los Angeles County has a really great exhibit called *Cats! Mild to Wild.* Click on Biology, and you will find how cats are built, how they use their claws, teeth, legs, and voices — and more!

www.kidsplanet.org
On *Kids' Planet* by Defenders of Wildlife you can play games and view the Web of Life story. You also can learn how to join other people in saving endangered wildlife.

www.epa.gov/students/ecosyste.htm
The *Environmental Protection Agency Student Center* is a great place to learn about the places that cougars live, to see other endangered species and the places they live, and to find out what you can do to help protect wildlife and the Earth.

www.mortay.com/Cougar/Lion.shtml
The Mountain Lion is a site devoted to the cougar. It includes information about where cougars live, what they eat, how they hunt, and how many are left.

www.vrd.org/locator/subject.shtml#science
Do you have more questions about cougars? Try *Ask an Expert.* This site has scientists and naturalists who will help you find out whatever you need to know.

GLOSSARY

You can find these words on the pages listed. Reading a word in a sentence helps you understand it even better.

balance of nature (BAL-uhns of NAY-chur) — an idea of how all the animals and plants would affect each other's numbers if humans did not interfere 20

caribou (KAR-ah-boo) — a large deer, like a reindeer, with big antlers 16

cubs (KUHBZ) — big cats' babies 10, 12, 14, 20

den (DEN) — the place where big cats give birth, hide their cubs, and sometimes sleep 12

endangered (en-DAYN-jurd) — at risk of becoming extinct or dying out 16

habitats (HAB-uh-tats) — the natural places where a type of animal lives that gives it enough food and shelter 8, 18

jaguar (JAG-wahr) — the largest of the American wild cats, with black circles and spots on a yellow coat 6

mate (MAYT) — come together to make babies 10

predators (PRED-uh-turs) — animals that hunt other animals for food 12, 14

prey (PRAY) — animals that are hunted by other animals for food 14, 16, 18, 20

rodents (ROHD-uhnts) — small animals, like mice, rats, or squirrels, with large front teeth used for gnawing or nibbling 16

yowl (YOWL) — a long, sad-sounding cry or howl 18

INDEX